DYING WITH GRACE AND HOPE

Dr. S. Allen Foster

Desert Ministries, Inc.
P.O. Box 788, Palm Beach, FL 33480

DYING WITH GRACE AND HOPE

First Edition
© Copyright 2000 by
DESERT MINISTRIES, INC.
P. O. Box 788
Palm Beach, Florida 33480

ISBN 0-914733-27-3

Graphic Design and Printing By
Eagle Graphic Services
Fort Lauderdale, Florida

Dedication

I would like to dedicate this little book to the memory of Joseph C. Swaim, Jr., an outstanding attorney, dedicated churchman, board member of Desert Ministries, true Christian gentleman and good friend. He was the Clerk of Session at Southminster Presbyterian Church in Pittsburgh, PA, at the time of his death from a brain tumor. Joe died as he lived, with gentle grace and genuine Christian hope. It was my honor and joy to have been his pastor and friend for 14 years.

> *"But we do not want you to be uninformed, brothers and sisters, about those who have died, so that you may not grieve as others do who have no hope. For since we believe that Jesus died and rose again, even so, through Jesus, God will bring with him those who have died."*
>
> (1 Thessalonians 4:13-14)

A Word From The Publisher

Dear Friend and Reader:

We are pleased at Desert Ministries to bring you this useful book by a Pastor who has often been there to help individuals and families on the final journey. Dr. Foster is beloved to his members and friends, but especially those to whom he has ministered with grace and hope.

This is a fine example of the kind of books and booklets we sponsor for laity and clergy who are going through the various crisis times of life. At the close, you will find a list of some other DMI books on related topics. We will make them available to you on request.

We are most grateful to the Robert and Mary Weisbrod Foundation, National City Center, Pittsburgh, Pennsylvania, for the gift of funds to enable us to publish this book.

Meanwhile, God bless you and keep you in His care.

Cordially,

Rev. Dr. Richard M. Cromie
President, Desert Ministries, Inc.

Table of Contents

Acknowledgements

I would like to express by deep appreciation to my administrative assistant, Glenda Arthur, who worked on this manuscript through several drafts and to my wife, Miriam, who encouraged me to write it.

Introduction

Why do we resist facing the reality of death, whether our own or that of others whom we love dearly? Is it fear of the physical, emotional and spiritual pain of dying? Is it fear of personal extinction on the "far side?" Is it fear of facing God's judgment? Perhaps it is a combination of these and others issues.

The reasons we avoid facing death until it is actually thrust upon us vary from person to person. The tendency to avoid this inevitable reality, however, seems almost universal. Few of us openly embrace death unless it is inevitable, and even then, denial is an essential stage of the process.[1]

I seem to be something of a rarity in this regard. Perhaps it has to do with the fact that I lost both of my parents early in life, one after years of struggle with heart disease and the other after a yearlong battle with cancer.

Then came my own wrestling match with death in my early 30s. After spending two months in the hospital and coming close to death several times, I slowly regained my health. These experiences made a strong imprint on me and brought me a strange blessing, since I am now a pastor who has ministered to hundreds who have died and to their loved ones. I have discovered a very special ministry in helping people die with grace and hope.

While this book is largely based on my personal experiences, some of what I share I have learned from books and seminars. For more than 30 years, I have stood by the side of dying parishioners every week, and for months afterwards with their grieving loved ones. I seek to share what I have learned for the sake of all of us who must face our own death, as well as family, friends and clergy who must minister to the dying. Consequently, I have all three audiences in mind as I write. I am also writing about the entire process of dying and grief, for this is one existential reality and cannot be divided in real life. I certainly do not pretend to know it all, but my hope is that these little lessons will help you respond to one of life's deepest events with grace and hope.[2]

DYING WITH GRACE AND HOPE

Sudden Death

Some people face death unexpectedly. A sudden heart attack or accident can take someone from us with little or no warning. I have been through this trauma with many people over the years and have discovered that the grieving process can be especially difficult for the loved ones who are left behind. There is no chance to prepare yourself as there is with a long, terminal illness. There is no chance to grieve in anticipation of death. Those who help and minister to the loved ones of a "sudden death victim" need to develop a special understanding of how this grief differs from the grief of those who are able to let go slowly.

I remember one woman who suddenly lost her husband of many years to a heart attack one Saturday. He had said goodbye that morning, and it had seemed like any other. However, he left and never returned.

His wife found her grief most difficult to bear. Although she experienced an initial outpouring of emotion, she then went into a long period of emotional numbness. She was in an extended state of shock, and more than a year passed before she could feel the other emotions of grief, which include guilt, anger, profound sadness, depression and almost unbearable loneliness.[3]

She stayed away from church for more than two years, because she could not bear the memories of sharing a special place in the sanctuary with her husband. Music especially upset her and caused uncontrollable emotional outbursts. She found this a very embarrassing problem.

I had to walk a very gentle line with this lovely woman, who was a private person. On the one hand, I tried to give her the space she needed to grieve in her own way on her own schedule. On the other hand, I found excuses to drop by her house periodically in order to encourage her to face her grief openly and work through all the painful stages.

In her own time, she was able to move beyond shock and numbness to the other stages of grief. Sometimes she bounced from anger to depression to loneliness and back again, and I assured her that it was normal.

Some people experience one or two aspects of grief very profoundly and hardly feel the others at all. I have learned through the years that that is okay, too, so long as they continue to work through their grief and do not attempt to avoid it.

I have likewise discovered that there is a uniqueness in the way we grieve. Although we must work through all the stages of grief, how we do it depends on our personality and our relationship with our loved one. I knew one widow who was in her mid-60s when her husband died. I never saw her show any sign of grief in public, and it worried me. I was a young pastor and was concerned that she wasn't doing her "grief work." Finally, I had a private conversation with her in which I learned that she was, indeed, working through the various stages. However, she was doing it behind closed doors.

We only need to be concerned when our grieving loved ones or friends try to avoid their grief work altogether, perhaps through busyness, extended seclusion or marrying again too quickly. Unfortunately, if we do not work through it, it will show itself in the form of emotional problems or physical ailments later on. Avoiding grief will cause serious difficulties for a hasty new marriage, as well.

With these provisos in mind, remember we will grieve in a fashion that reflects our unique personality and personal loss. Consequently, when you help people who are grieving, you must allow them to be themselves. Don't push anyone to grieve the way you think you would or they should. Likewise, remember that after a sudden death, the grieving person may take longer to come out of shock and complete the grief work than if their loved one had died slowly.

Slow Death

Let us now turn to the process of letting go slowly. When someone learns that he has a terminal illness, life suddenly changes not only for him, but also for his family. A journey begins that will take them over many strange and rocky roads into that valley of deep darkness we call death (Psalm 23:1-4).

How can we help prepare the way for the dying person and his loved ones? Like grief, there are some common features that are helpful to understand. Still, each person's journey will have unique aspects, thanks to the type and course of the disease and the person's own personality. No one can be totally prepared for death, but it helps to make any preparations we can.

Dying slowly can be a terrible process to endure. At a physical level, dying means that the human body progressively shuts down. As death approaches, more and more physical problems and changes take place. For example, a dying person eventually loses a desire to eat. Food no longer tastes good and may cause discomfort, nausea and vomiting. This is very difficult to watch, and there is a natural tendency for loved ones to try to coax the dying one to eat beyond capability or comfort level.

5

It is far wiser to ask the doctor what to expect and to listen to what your loved one says. Your loved one probably knows what is happening in his own body. Remember that you are there to comfort, help and understand. Be sensitive to the real and expressed needs of the dying person and to sound medical advice. Do not force your own agenda. What you think is best may actually reflect your own anxieties. You can talk these out with a pastor or family member.

As the body continues to shut down, the dying person may sleep more and more. When this happens, less distress and pain are felt. From time to time, the patient may need to have a sip of water or a swabbing of the mouth for comfort's sake. Be a comforter as needed. It is a gentle, but important, ministry you can perform that will speak volumes of your love.

As the process continues, fluid may accumulate in the lungs or back of the throat. Breaths may have a watery, rattle-like sound to them. Be sure your doctor gives the necessary medications for secretions and orders that your loved one is turned every few hours to prevent fluids from collecting in the lungs and to avert bed sores. However, suctioning of the lungs and throat may be of limited value toward the end and may actually be uncomfortable. Discuss appropriate action with a compassionate doctor and follow that advice instead of your own instincts. The comfort of your loved one is always the goal.

The kidneys and bowels will also shut down. Urine will lessen in amount, but increase in concentration. A catheter may be necessary to aid the voiding process. Constipation may develop and help may be required to clear the bowels. Eventually, most people lose control of their bowels and bladder as their muscles relax. Keeping your loved one as dry and clean as possible will enhance his dignity. Consult your doctor about treating constipation and using a catheter. The doctor has surely been through this many times and can give you the best advice.

As death draws closer, the senses will also start to shut down. Vision will become blurred, speech limited and sleep deeper and more frequent. At this stage, many people think that the dying person cannot hear conversations around him. In reality, hearing is the last sense to go, and a dying person may clearly hear inappropriate things said by family and friends. When I was very sick, I went through a period when I could not communicate, but I could hear others' voices clearly. Consequently, it is quite important to continue gentle touching and speaking words of love and prayer, even when a dying person does not respond. These are terribly important. Since you do not know what your loved one can hear or feel, you should surround him with love and prayer to the end.

Near the end of life, other vital organs begin to fail. As the body attempts to conserve blood flow to the most important organs, the hands and feet may feel cold. Skin color may become pale. There will be a change in the rate and depth of breathing. At times, it may seem as if the dying person is not breathing at all. Suddenly, he will take another shallow breath. It is reassuring to understand that the dying person is not suffocating and is usually unconscious. The body is simply preparing to shut down totally.[4]

Although the clinical aspects of physical death can be significant, what often worries the dying person and his loved ones most is whether death will be painful. In general, this depends on the disease. However, pain can now be managed effectively, thanks to modern hospice care. It is no longer necessary to die in pain. If your regular doctor does not understand this or seems unsympathetic to your concerns, locate a hospice as quickly as possible. You will find hospice workers extremely helpful with all aspects of dying with dignity, including pain management. Having the assistance of hospice will relieve unnecessary anxiety on everyone's part.

The Emotional Challenges of Dying

The emotional challenges of a slow death are equally important to understand. What does the dying person feel inside? How much will he be able to share with you? How important is this? Are there any guidelines for clergy and loved ones seeking to assist this emotional process?

The best way to help you understand is to relate a personal story. When I was a young graduate student living in Edinburgh, Scotland, I developed a serious intestinal disease. It was progressive, and I was hospitalized for two months. During this time, I lost one-third of my body weight, had many complications and nearly lost my life. I came to believe I was dying, because despite the excellent medical care offered at this teaching hospital of the University of Edinburgh, I went downhill.

I can remember thinking, "This can't be happening to me. I am only 32 years old. My wife and three small children are alone in a foreign land. I have to provide for them. Moreover, I have given my life to God to serve as a Christian minister. This can't be happening to me." But it was.

Subsequently, I became angry and anxious. I was upset with God and this untimely turn of events. I was frustrated that my life was being cut short, and there was nothing I could do. I grew more anxious with each passing day. I became concerned about the future suffering I would endure, the bodily indignities and the end of my dreams for this life. My prayers seemed to go nowhere, and I began to doubt if God was there at all.

For a while I tried bargaining with God. When I awakened in the wee hours of the night in the hospital ward surrounded by the ill and dying, I would pray saying, "Oh God, if you just make me well I will do…" I promised God the moon. But the bargaining didn't work, and I grew more anxious as my physical condition worsened.

Finally, I became quite sad. At this point I also accepted what appeared to be inevitable. Then I remember waking very early as the sun was coming up in the summer sky over Scotland and simply praying, "Oh God, I give up my struggle, but I do trust your love whether I live or die." Almost at once, a sense of profound peace set in. Why had I been so slow to reach this stage? The presence of God seemed almost palpable in that hospital ward.

When I read the writings of Elisabeth Kubler-Ross a few years later, I came to realize that although I had lived through that ordeal, I had actually experienced all the normal stages of dying.[5]   I had been given a very special gift: Although it had been a frightening and painful time, I knew what it was like to face death, not only in the physical sense, but in the emotional and spiritual sense, as well. God wanted me to use this knowledge as a pastor. Of this I was sure.

Through the recent hospice movement, we have learned a great deal more about the variety of ways people let go slowly. We have learned how dying varies emotionally according to our unique personalities and life experiences. We now know why certain patients seem to get stuck at a given stage of the dying process. Likewise, we have learned how loved ones, ministers and doctors can help a dying person to break free and move toward full acceptance of the coming event.

Some people experience tremendous emotional growth in their final weeks and months of life. Others stagnate. Some people carry out final, personal tasks, while others give up and don't seem to care. Some work through their relationships with loved ones, forgiving and being forgiven for old mistakes and hurtful events in the past. Some grow to new depths of love and self-giving, even as life ebbs away, while others retreat behind walls of anger, denial or bitterness. However, the blessing of a slow death is the opportunity it affords the dying person and his loved ones to grow emotionally in the last precious weeks of life.[6]

Those who die the best deaths use these opportunities to take care of their emotional affairs and say goodbye with deepened love.[7] Don't let emotional hang-ups or past failures stop you from doing your final relationship work. This will be your last chance.

I will never forget a delightful woman I pastored in a former congregation. Although I was not particularly drawn to her flamboyant personality at first, when her husband suddenly died, she dealt with her anger beautifully. She went to his grave periodically to "tell him off" for abandoning her and God, too, for allowing him to die. In this manner, she dealt with the anger in her grief in a constructive manner.

A short time later, when she was diagnosed with cancer herself, she continued to pursue life to the fullest. I went to see her one day after she came home from the hospital only to discover that she and her college-aged son had taken a trip to Antarctica! Before she died, she visited every continent, working in the trips between hospitalizations. In the final days before she fell into a coma, she spent hours on the phone putting things right with relatives who lived far away. This wonderful woman managed to die well, because she took care of her emotional affairs in the last chapter of her life. My advice is that we all find a way to do likewise in the manner that suits us best.

Let me add one word of caution here for overly zealous loved ones. If you have a personal need to share something deep, perhaps some long-buried thoughts and emotions, you may try to force your dying loved one to open up. But don't mistake your needs for those of the dying person. While it may be okay for you to openly express what <u>you</u> need to say, you should not project your needs onto your dying loved one. Also, be aware that you might not get the response you hoped for or expected. Be sensitive to your loved one and express yourself as wisely, openly and gently as possible.

On the other hand, if you genuinely sense that your dying loved one wants to communicate some hidden, unspoken matter, open the door gently with a leading question or two, such as, "How are you feeling today? I sensed there was something you wanted to say yesterday, but it never got said. Was I wrong?" Don't force the issue. If your loved one really wants to talk, he will open up. If not, wait. In a few days, when you least expect it, that unspoken matter will likely emerge with true emotional healing power. If it is never said, that may be okay, too. It may have been your agenda and not your loved one's, so let it go.

If, however, your loved one gets stuck in a frightening stage of the grieving process and can't let go of anger or bitterness, you may want to seek some professional help. Some clergy and many hospice professionals understand this tricky problem and know what to do. Anger can be very scary, especially in someone you love. Moreover, if that anger cannot be worked through into a state of sadness and true acceptance of death, it can ruin the last opportunity you both will have to express deep love and say your final goodbyes.[8]

The patient may also experience some confusion toward the end that can easily cause misunderstandings. I recall one woman who was sure that her car keys were hanging on the wall in her hospital room. Her daughter tried to convince her mother otherwise, but this only made the woman more agitated. I simply went to the ostensible location of the imaginary keys, took them off the imaginary hook, and laid them on the nightstand beside the women's bed. She calmed down immediately. Someone had listened to her. Try to enter the patient's mind as much as possible, even when the altered reality makes no sense to you. Listen, be sensitive, flexible and loving.

If your loved one survives weeks or months with a terminal illness, you may witness periods of lucidity mixed with periods of agitation and confusion. This is normal. Go with the flow, taking one day at a time. You will be amazed how calming your flexible attitude will be to both of you.

In the final days, you can expect your loved one to withdraw more and more and to limit the time you share as sleep increases. This can be very difficult for family and loved ones who sense the need for a final goodbye. You may need to do some real grieving at this point, before the end comes. During such a time, it is okay to simply sit in silence or to step aside for a good cry of your own. Although silence can be unsettling, it is sometimes necessary and the best thing that you can do. To chatter on when a dying person is grieving is insensitive and unloving. The sound of silence toward the end can actually speak words of love.

The Spiritual Dimension

In our secular culture, it is very common to address the physical and emotional aspects of dying, while ignoring the spiritual dimensions. I consider this a sad state of affairs, for I have discovered from pastoral experience that genuine faith can make an enormous difference in the way we die. Moreover, I have repeatedly heard from those with little or no faith that they envy people who face death with genuine faith, whose final days are filled with hope and grace. They recognize that it brings a sense of peace.

A solid faith does many things for someone who is dying. For example, one of the most common experiences of dying is wrestling with a sense of hopelessness. People wonder, "Did my life really count for anything? Did it have meaning? Will it all be wiped out and quickly forgotten?" These are haunting questions. Dr. Victor Frankl, the brilliant and insightful psychiatrist who lived through a Nazi death camp experience, discovered that those who survived the death camp were not necessarily physically strong, but were spiritually strong. They had discovered a genuine meaning to their existence.[9] The advantage of a strong Christian faith is that it assures us that our earthly life does have mean-

17

ing and will be remembered by God and many others for eternity. What a great antidote for hopelessness!

Another common fear is that of personal extinction. It is the fear that the dying person's unique personality will vanish at death. Christian faith puts that fear to rest. God assures us that in Christ we will be called forth from death into eternal life, where we will maintain our personal identity. Christ's life is the model of hope for us. Moreover, since heaven is about growing in a love relationship with God and others, this opens up tremendous opportunities in the future. It's the peace in knowing that the kind of reconciliation, forgiveness and growth in love that so many people discover in their final days on earth can — and will — go on and on.

On the other hand, some people fear death because they see God as an angry judge, rather than the loving Father that Jesus described. For such people, death means facing judgment and punishment. A wise pastor will allow such fears to surface, then slowly lead the dying person to discover that there is no hidden God behind Jesus' gracious back. Fear of God's judgment is meant to lead us to repent, to change and trust in the true and loving God. If someone is feeling guilty about a life badly lived, or was reared in a largely negative theology, the discovery of God's love can bring true hope in the final days of earthly life. Remember the repentant thief on the cross? Christ still ministers to such souls today through people such as you and me.

I remember an experience I had about 12 years ago that made a deep impression on me. We were back in Scotland for the Summer Institute of Theology at St. Andrews University. I asked one of the speakers about a former teacher named Professor James S. Stewart. He had taught the New Testament for more than twenty years at the University of Edinburgh, as well as being the Queen's chaplain in Scotland, moderator of the Church of Scotland and one of the 20th century's greatest preachers. I learned that he was living in a Roman Catholic retirement community at the edge of Edinburgh, where the nuns gave him excellent, compassionate care. His wife had died and he was alone at age 90.

My wife and I went to visit him. We introduced ourselves and reminded him of the 1960s, when I was a student in the University of Edinburgh. He immediately "clicked-in." (His long-term memory was still quite good, although his short-term memory was gone).

After a nice conversation, we revealed that we had returned to Scotland to celebrate our 25th wedding anniversary. He then asked if he could offer a prayer for us and for our church. Of course, we were delighted. His prayer was one of the most beautiful I have ever heard. We then inquired about his daily life, and I will never forget his answer. He smiled and said, "I'm just waiting here to venture forth into God's next great adventure." I never knew a man who had a stronger belief in the God of the Resurrection, and it surely showed. James S. Stewart died with hope, grace and tremendous faith.

Several modern medical studies support what this personal story illustrates: that people of genuine faith suffer less from the fear of death than do those who have little or no faith. Some, like Professor Stewart, seem to welcome death at a profound level. Why? Because they see death not as an end, but as God's next great adventure.[10]

Cardinal Joseph Bernardin of Chicago visibly demonstrated this positive approach to death to our generation and our secular society. While dying with pancreatic cancer, Cardinal Bernardin openly talked about his physical, emotional and spiritual struggles as death approached. He was an honest man of faith. He shared his humanity and struggles, but continued his life of Christian service until his strength finally gave out.

Thirteen days before his death, Cardinal Bernardin finished the manuscript of his last book. He then wrote these powerful words:

As I write these final words, my heart is filled with joy. I am at peace...I will soon experience new life in a different way. Although I do not know what to expect in the afterlife, I do know that just as God has called me to serve him to the best of my ability throughout my life on earth, he is now calling me home. Many people have asked me to tell them about heaven and the afterlife. I sometimes smile at the request because I do not know any more than they do. Yet, when one young man asked if I looked forward to being united with God and all those who have gone before me, I made a connection to something I said earlier in this book.

The first time I traveled with my mother and sister to my parent's homeland of Tonadico di Primiero, in Northern Italy, I felt as if I had been there before. After years of looking through my mother's photo albums, I knew the mountains, the land, the houses, the people. As soon as we entered the valley, I said, "My God, I know this place. I am home." Somehow I think crossing from this life into eternal life will be similar. I will be home.[11]

Helping people claim the peace, hope and grace of Christian faith in the midst of their dying is the special privilege of the clergy. However, anyone of genuine faith can help. I have discovered that what I call "the ministry of constant presence" is most important. Visit the dying person regularly. It is not necessary to stay long, unless the patient indicates a desire for a longer conversation. These short visits respect the declining strength and patience of the dying person. However, the frequency of the visits tells the person that you really do care and will not abandon him. Frequent visits also build up a bond over time that longer, more infrequent visits do not. This bond allows a dying person to open up and express his fears, questions and doubts.

I recall one man I visited when he was dying of cancer. He was a neighbor and a friend, but not a church member. He was a scientist and had lots of scientifically based questions and doubts. Over some months of my brief visits, this man started to open up. I accepted his doubts and struggles. He then wanted some Christian reading material that would address his personal and existential questions. Soon, he asked for reading material that was devotional in nature. Finally, he asked me to pray for him and with him.

If you are a genuine, steady, sensitive, listening, Christian friend to a dying person, you may have the opportunity to share that person's most pressing questions, issues I call "Gethsemane struggles." They help genuine, deep faith to emerge. Patience, sensitivity, perseverance and true caring are the keys to helping a dying person discover, rediscover or deepen their faith in the final days of this earthly journey. What a privilege it is to be welcomed into this most intimate time in a person's life! Do it with God's grace and as a genuine expression of God's love as we have come to know it in Jesus Christ.

The Funeral and Beyond

This chapter is for grieving families and clergy who minister to dying patients. It's for everyone who understands that the clergy can be with you not only as death approaches, but also beyond death. After the doctors, nurses and hospice workers are gone, it is the clergy who continue ministering to loved ones throughout the grieving process, no matter how long it takes. The death of a loved one and your own grief are one existential reality, and clergy are often the only ones who see the "whole picture."

This concept was brought home to me in my first church. One of our members had just died, and I came into the room to comfort his wife. The doctor looked greatly relieved to see me and quickly disappeared through a side door. He had done all he could do. I understood it was now my responsibility to see this woman through the grieving process. All others had vanished. This is usually the reality of the situation.

The first part of the grieving process is preparing for the funeral or memorial service. I generally meet with the family in their home (or in my study) within a short time after the death occurs. I outline what I generally do at a funeral and then invite them to share any special music, readings and scriptures they would like to include. This helps to personalize the service, so that it truly reflects the beloved's unique life. Then I ask the family and loved ones to share their personal memories of what made their loved one so special. This not only helps me to write a very personal eulogy (or "celebration of life," as I prefer to call it), but it gives the family a therapeutic opportunity to laugh and cry together as they share their special memories. It is an important time of "healing through sharing."

When my father died, a good friend at seminary who was studying pastoral counseling at a graduate level did this for me, and I found it amazingly helpful. In my own pastoral experience, hundreds of people have told me that this sharing time was extremely helpful to them as well. It is one of the first steps in grieving openly and in a healthy way.

I usually conclude the funeral service with a brief meditation on eternal life and a pastoral prayer committing the deceased and the family left behind into the Hands of God. I feel that this pattern provides a funeral service that is at once scriptural and prayerful, personal and hopeful. We end the service on a note of hope and grace, assured that we are all held in the Hand of God until that grand reunion at God's throne of grace, when He will wipe away the last tear from the last eye, because death is no more (Revelation 21:4).

Naturally, some people are more open to this ministry than others. Consequently, it certainly helps if the pastor has maintained a positive and sincere ministry to the dying person throughout the final illness, the funeral and on into the grieving process. The key word is "trust." If you are trusted as genuine and sincere, people will be open to you more quickly.

My visits to the bereaved are generally longer in duration than my quick, but frequent, visits to the dying. However, I usually start with a brief visit within weeks after the funeral. Family members may not be ready to do any serious grief work yet, but this visit tells them that they have not been forgotten and establishes an atmosphere of caring in which the real grief work will be able to unfold in the months ahead.

While I have touched on the grief process at several points in this small book, I do not intend to detail the role of the clergy at each step of the way. There are a number of excellent books available to guide anyone seeking to minister to those in grief. (The person you are helping through the grief process might also need to be referred to someone with more training than you have or to a grief recovery group. This is genuine help you can provide).

What I want to emphasize here, however,

is that the pastor is likely to be the sole person who will see family members not only through the death of their beloved, but through their own grief as well. Consequently, it is vital that clergy understand their role and accept responsibility for the whole process on a physical, emotional and spiritual level. It is a unique and often difficult job, but for me there is no ministry that is more important or satisfying, for it touches people at the deepest levels of human existence.

Two additional notes need mentioning. First, I feel it is absolutely necessary that pastors be thoroughly versed in grief counseling. You can prepare yourself with courses, seminars, books and tapes provided by the experts in this field. Only if you are knowledgeable will you be familiar with the entire grief process and know what to do if something unexpected occurs.

On a final note, I would like to underscore the value of "genuine presence." If people sense that you are really "there" for them, and that you truly care and listen, they will open up and you will be able to help them. It is very easy for a grieving person to spot a pastor who only pretends to be interested. At this point, the grieving person will clam up. This, in fact, may set back the grieving process considerably and make it much harder for that person to trust others who might genuinely help.

It is a high privilege to be allowed to share

some of life's most intimate moments with dying and grieving "fellow strugglers." Consequently, clergy must seek to provide this special pastoral care to the very best of their ability.

Conclusion

I close with a comment I once heard from Professor James S. Stewart. I often share it at funerals or with someone in grief. Stewart said, "When you pray and your faith is strong, you are holding onto the left hand of the Risen Christ. Your loved one who has gone before you into eternal life now holds on to the right hand of the Risen Christ. In the meantime, Christ is your bridge. Hold fast!"

Epilogue

It is my high privilege to have been prepared for this special ministry to dying people and their loved ones. It is a joy to grow in this ministry every week, as I have for the past 30 years. It is my prayer now that this little book will help you, or help you to help others, in this difficult time of life we must all face. After all, death is a doorway that we must assist others to pass through and then go through ourselves.

May this poetic epitaph written by C. S. Lewis for his beloved wife, Helen Joy Davidman, serve as a beacon for all of you who seek to help others die, and then die yourself with grace and hope:

Here the whole world (stars, water, air and field, and forest, as they were reflected in a single mind)

*Like cast-off clothes was left behind
In ashes yet with Hope that she,
Re-born from holy poverty,
In Lenten lands, hereafter may
Resume them on her Easter Day.*[12]

Suggestions for Further Reading

Albom, Mitch. Tuesdays with Morrie. New York: Doubleday, 1997

Bernardin, Joseph Cardinal. The Gift of Peace. New York: Doubleday, 1998.

Byock, Ira, M.D. Dying Well: Peace and Possibilities at the End of Life. New York: Riverhead, 1997.

Callanan, Maggie and Kelley, Patricia. Final Gifts: Understanding the Special Awareness, Needs, and Communications of the Dying. New York: Bantam, 1997.

Frankl, Victor. Man's Search for Meaning: An Introduction to Logotherapy. New York: Simon & Shuster, 1959.

Kubler-Ross, Elisabeth. On Death and Dying. New York: Macmillan, 1969.

Kubler-Ross, Elisabeth. Questions and Answers on Death and Dying. New York: Collier, 1974.

Levine, Stephen. A Year to Live. New York: Bell Tower, 1997.

Lewis, C. S. A Grief Observed. New York: Bantam, 1976.

Matthews, Dale A., M.D. The Faith Factor. New York: Penguin, 1999.

Sigrist, Deborah. What to Expect as a Loved One's Death Draws Near. St. Meinrad: Abbey Press, 1999.

Spiro, Howard M.; Curnen, Mary G. McCrea and Wandel, Lee Palmer, Eds. Facing Death. New Haven: Yale University Press, 1996.

Walmsley, Lesley Ed. C.S. Lewis on Grief. Nashville: Thomas Nelson, 1998.

Westberg, Granger E. Good Grief. Philadelphia: Fortress Press, 1971.

Sources

[1] Elisabeth Kübler-Ross, On Death and Dying (New York: Macmillan, 1969), pp38-49.

[2] Masculine pronouns have been used throughout this booklet for ease of reading and not because of a lack of sensitivity to issues of sexism in language. I trust the reader will understand.

[3] See Granger E. Westberg, Good Grief (Philadelphia: Fortress Press, 1971).

[4] Deborah Sigrist, What to Expect as a Loved One's Death Draws Near (St. Meinrad: Abbey Press, 1999) p. 2-4.

[5] Elisabeth Kübler-Ross, Questions and Answers on Death and Dying (New York: Collier, 1974), pp. 1-33.

[6] See Ira Byock, Dying Well: Peace and Possibilities at the End of Life (New York: Riverhead, 1997); Maggie Callanan, and Patricia Kelley: Understanding the Special Awareness, Needs, and Communications of the Dying (New York: Bantam, 1997).

[7] Mitch Albom, Tuesdays with Morrie (New York: Doubleday, 1997).

[8] Ira Byock, op. Cit: pp. 59-84.

[9] Victor F. Frankl, Man's Search for Meaning: An Introduction to Logotherapy (New York: Simon & Shuster-1959)

[10] Dale A. Matthews, The Faith Factor (New York: Penquin, 1999) pp. 161-164.

[11] Joseph Cardinal Bernardin, The Gift of Peace (New York: Doubleday, 1998), pp. 151-2.

[12] Lesley Walmsley Ed. C. S. Lewis on Grief (Nashville: Thomas Nelson, 1998), p. 9.

OTHER
DESERT MINISTRIES, INC.
PUBLICATIONS

How To Live With Cancer
Como Vivir Con Cancer
Christ Will See You Through *(Revised and Enlarged)*
When You Lose Someone You Love
The Future Is Now
The Rhapsody of Scripture
When Alzheimer's Disease Strikes
Prayers Against Depression
God's Promises & My Needs
How To Help An Alcoholic
You Now Have Custody Of You
My Adventures With Mankind
Humor and Healing
Reflections On Suicide
When A Child Dies
Who Really Listens When I Speak?

Desert Ministries, Inc.
P.O. Box 788
Palm Beach, FL 33480-0788

(561) 832-0207
Fax: (561) 832-0279

Website: http://www.desmin.org